Dedication

To my beloved mother,

May C. Brown

Though you are no longer with me in this world, your spirit continues to guide and inspire me every single day. You taught me, by word and example, the power of kindness, the importance of loving others, and the strength that comes from treating every person with respect and compassion. Your unwavering belief in my potential, your encouragement to always strive for greatness, and your gentle wisdom have shaped every part of who I am—both as a trader and as a human being.

Your love is the foundation on which I build my dreams. This book is dedicated to you, with endless gratitude and love. May your legacy of kindness and inspiration live on in every page, and in every life I'm able to touch.

— Hank

Henry "Hank" Brown
MASTERING THE MIND: EMOTIONAL DISCIPLINE IN TRADING

This book is designed to provide concepts and suggestions in regard to the subject matter covered. It is sold with the understanding that neither the author nor the publisher is engaged in rendering legal, accounting, or other professional services. If legal advice or other expert assistance is required, the services of a competent professional person should be sought. This book is based on real world experience and in no way is the author or publisher a professional psychologist or financial advisor. This book is for educational purposes only.

MASTERING THE MIND: Emotional Discipline in Trading

Cover art and design by Henry "Hank" Brown

ISBN: 9798218710965

Table of Contents

Henry "Hank" Brown
MASTERING THE MIND: EMOTIONAL DISCIPLINE IN TRADING

Introduction

Why Psychology Matters More Than Strategy

"Markets expose who you are. Master yourself –
and you master the market."

When most people start their trading journey, they
obsess over finding the perfect strategy—searching for
the right indicators, patterns, or systems that will
unlock consistent profits. Yet, if you ask any seasoned
trader what truly separates winners from losers, the
answer almost always points to one thing: psychology.

While a sound strategy is essential, it's your mindset—
how you handle fear, greed, stress, and uncertainty—
that determines your long-term success. The markets
are unpredictable and often irrational, but it's your
emotional responses to wins, losses, and missed
opportunities that shape your results far more than any
technical setup ever could.

Think about it: Why do so many traders abandon a
proven system after a losing streak? Why do some cut
winners short out of fear, or let losses spiral out of
control hoping for a reversal? The answer isn't a lack of
knowledge—it's the struggle to master the mental
game.

Henry "Hank" Brown
MASTERING THE MIND: EMOTIONAL DISCIPLINE IN TRADING

Trading psychology is the invisible force behind every decision you make. It governs your discipline, resilience, and ability to stick to your plan when the pressure is on. Without a strong psychological foundation, even the best strategy will fail—because success in trading isn't just about what you know, but how you think, feel, and act under real market conditions.

In the chapters ahead, you'll discover why mastering your mind is the greatest edge you can develop—and how building emotional discipline will elevate every aspect of your trading journey.

Key Points:

- Most traders know what to do, but can't consistently do it
- Emotional sabotage (fear, FOMO, revenge) kills more traders than bad entries
- This book will give you real-life, reflection prompts, and actionable frameworks

LOGICAL TRADER	EMOTIONAL TRADER
Analytical	Impulsive
Sticks to a plan	Chases the market
Objective	Subjective
Disciplined	Inconsistent

CHAPTER 1

FEAR OF LOSING

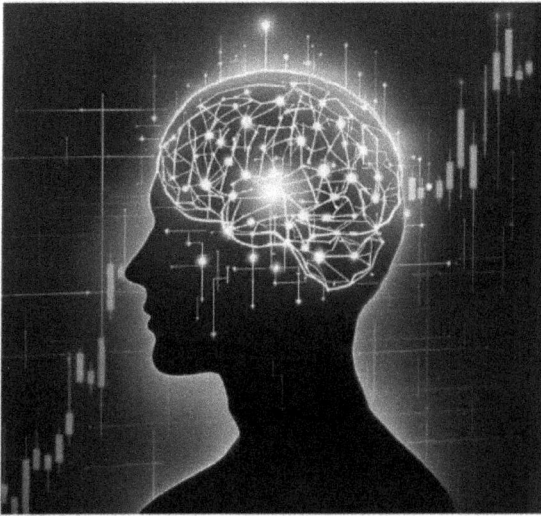

CHAPTER 1: Fear of Losing

What Is the Fear of Losing?

Fear of losing is one of the most powerful and universal emotions every trader faces. At its core, it's the anxiety or dread that comes with the possibility of making a losing trade—whether that loss is financial, emotional, or psychological. For many traders, especially beginners, this fear can be paralyzing. It can prevent you from entering trades, cause you to exit positions prematurely, or lead to a cycle of hesitation and self-doubt that sabotages your progress.

The fear of losing isn't just about the money—it's about what the loss represents. It can feel like a blow to your confidence, your competence, or even your identity as a successful trader. If left unchecked, this fear becomes a major barrier to growth and consistency in the markets.

Why Does Fear of Losing Happen?

1. Natural Human Instincts

Humans are hardwired to avoid pain and seek pleasure. In trading, a loss feels like pain—sometimes even like a personal failure. Our brains are designed to protect us from danger, so the fear of losing is a natural response to the risk involved in trading.

2. Attachment to Outcomes

Many traders become emotionally attached to the outcome of each trade, measuring their self-worth or skill by whether a single trade wins or loses. This attachment amplifies the fear of being wrong.

3. Lack of Experience or Confidence

New traders, or those who have recently suffered big losses, often lack the confidence that comes from a track record of following a plan. This uncertainty fuels the fear of making another mistake.

4. Over-Leverage and High Stakes

Risking too much on any given trade increases the emotional stakes. The more you stand to lose, the greater your fear becomes.

5. Past Traumas

A string of losses or a particularly painful loss can leave a psychological scar, making you overly cautious or anxious about future trades.

How Fear of Losing Shows Up in Trading

Fear of losing can manifest in many subtle (and not-so-subtle) ways in your trading decisions:

- **Paralysis by Analysis:** Overthinking every detail and missing trade opportunities because you're afraid to pull the trigger.

- **Premature Exits:** Closing trades too early at the first sign of a small loss or even a small profit, just to avoid "the pain" of a bigger loss.

- **Avoiding Trades Altogether:** Sitting on the sidelines, watching setups pass by, and convincing yourself it's "safer not to trade."

- **Micromanaging Positions:** Constantly adjusting stops or targets, unable to let the trade play out.

- **Second-Guessing:** Entering a trade, then immediately doubting your decision and exiting with little or no movement.

The Cost of Fear of Losing

While fear is a natural part of trading, letting it control your actions can be costly:

- **Missed Opportunities:** You miss out on profitable trades because you're afraid to enter.

- **Inconsistent Results:** Exiting too early or hesitating leads to inconsistent execution and unpredictable results.

- **Erosion of Confidence:** Each time you let fear dictate your actions, your self-trust erodes, making it even harder to act decisively in the future.

- **Stunted Growth:** You never develop the skills or confidence to execute your plan, so your learning curve is much slower.

The Psychology Behind the Fear

Understanding the psychological roots of this fear is key to overcoming it:

- **Loss Aversion:** Studies show we feel the pain of loss about twice as strongly as we feel the pleasure of gain. This makes us naturally risk-averse.

- **Ego and Identity:** Many traders see a losing trade as a reflection of their intelligence or worth, rather than as just one outcome in a series.

- **Desire for Certainty:** The markets are uncertain by nature, but the human mind craves predictability. This mismatch creates ongoing anxiety.

Real-Life Example

Imagine you've just had a string of three losing trades. You spot a great setup that matches your plan, but the memory of those losses makes your heart race. You hesitate, watching the price action tick by. By the time you muster the courage to enter, the move is almost over—or you skip the trade entirely. Later, you see it would have been a winner, and your confidence drops even further. This cycle repeats until you're paralyzed by the fear of losing.

How to Overcome Fear of Losing: Practical Strategies

1. Accept Losses as Part of the Game

Every trader—no matter how experienced—takes losses. It's impossible to win 100% of the time. Start seeing losses as tuition for your trading education, not as failures.

2. Focus on Process, Not Outcomes

Shift your mindset from "I must win this trade" to "I must follow my plan." Judge your success by how well

you execute your process, not by the result of any single
trade.

3. Use Proper Position Sizing

Risk only a small, predetermined percentage of your
capital on each trade. Knowing that no single loss can
significantly hurt you will make it easier to act without
fear.

4. Develop and Trust Your Trading Plan

A clear, tested plan reduces uncertainty. The more you
trust your edge, the less you'll fear any individual
outcome.

5. Keep a Trading Journal

Record your trades, including your emotions and
decision-making process. Over time, you'll see that
following your plan—even when it leads to a loss—is the
real win.

6. Practice Mindfulness and Emotional Awareness

Notice when fear is creeping in. Take a few deep
breaths, step away from the screen if needed, and
remind yourself that your value as a trader isn't defined
by one trade.

7. Set Realistic Expectations

Understand that drawdowns and losing streaks are normal. Prepare for them mentally and financially.

8. Review Your Progress Regularly

Look back at your journal to see how you handled losses in the past. Celebrate your discipline and growth, not just your profits.

Final Thoughts

The fear of losing is a universal experience, but it doesn't have to control you. By accepting losses as part of the journey, focusing on your process, and building emotional resilience, you'll develop the confidence and consistency that set successful traders apart.

Remember:
You can't eliminate losses, but you can learn to manage your fear.
Mastering this skill is the foundation for long-term trading success.

Fear of Losing – Cheat Sheet

Emotional Behaviors:

- Hesitating on trades
- Micromanaging positions
- Closing winners too soon

Anecdote:

"After I experienced my first streak of losses, my next strategy-driven Long trade was before me – but I couldn't press buy. I didn't fear loss. I feared being wrong."

Solutions:

- Normalize losing (loss = cost of doing business)
- Limit daily dollar drawdown (e.g., 2% rule)
- Track fear triggers in a log

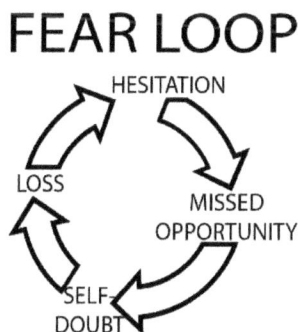

FEAR LOOP

HESITATION

LOSS

MISSED
OPPORTUNITY

SELF-
DOUBT

CHAPTER 2

REVENGE TRADING

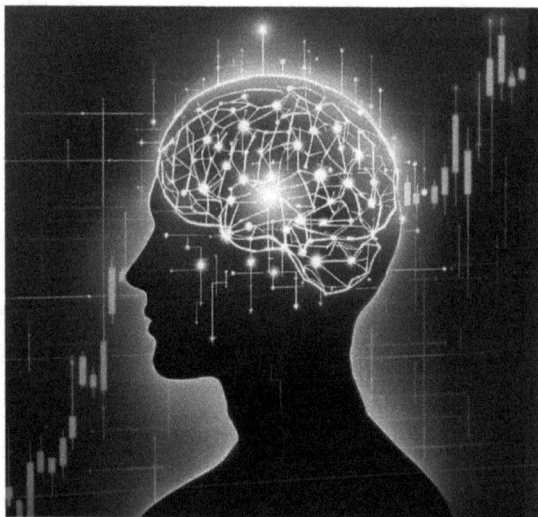

CHAPTER 2: Revenge Trading

What Is Revenge Trading?

Revenge trading is the emotional, impulsive act of trying to "win back" losses after a losing trade or series of losses. Instead of stepping back and evaluating what went wrong, a trader jumps back into the market—often with bigger positions, looser risk management, or trades outside of their strategy—driven by frustration, anger, or even desperation.

It's called "revenge" trading because the trader is, in essence, trying to get back at the market for causing pain. The focus shifts from following a sound plan to making up for losses as quickly as possible. Unfortunately, this almost always leads to more mistakes, bigger losses, and a destructive cycle that can wipe out trading accounts and confidence.

Why Does Revenge Trading Happen?

1. Emotional Response to Loss

Losses hurt. When a trade goes wrong, especially if it feels unfair or unexpected, it triggers strong emotions—anger, frustration, and sometimes shame. The urge to "get even" is a natural human reaction, but in trading, it's dangerous.

2. Ego and Identity

Many traders tie their self-worth to winning. A loss can feel like a personal failure, and revenge trading becomes a way to restore pride or prove something—to themselves or others.

3. Desire for Immediate Relief

The discomfort of a loss is intense. Revenge trading offers a (false) sense of control and the hope of instant recovery. The trader believes, "If I can just make this money back now, I'll feel better."

4. Cognitive Biases

- **Loss Aversion:** Losses feel twice as painful as gains feel good, so traders are more likely to take irrational risks to recover.

- **Overconfidence:** After a loss, some traders believe the next trade "has to" work out, leading to reckless decisions.

5. Lack of a Solid Plan

Without a clear, written trading plan—including rules for handling losses—it's easy to react emotionally instead of logically.

How Revenge Trading Shows Up

- **Doubling Down:** Increasing position size after a loss to recover quickly.

- **Overtrading:** Taking multiple rapid trades with little analysis.

- **Abandoning Strategy:** Entering setups you'd normally avoid, just to be "in the market."

- **Ignoring Risk Controls:** Moving stop-losses, removing them, or failing to use them at all.

- **Trading Out of Hours:** Jumping into trades outside your usual schedule or market times.

The Cost of Revenge Trading

Revenge trading almost always leads to more harm than good. Here's why:

- **Compounding Losses:** Instead of recovering, you often dig a deeper hole.

- **Emotional Burnout:** The stress and anxiety from chasing losses can lead to mental fatigue and poor health.

- **Loss of Discipline:** Every revenge trade erodes your ability to follow your plan in the future.

- **Account Blow-Ups:** Many traders have lost entire accounts in a single session due to revenge trading.

The Psychology Behind Revenge Trading

Understanding the emotional drivers is key to overcoming this destructive habit:

- **Fight or Flight:** After a loss, your brain's survival instincts kick in. You want to "fight back" against the pain.

- **Short-Term Focus:** Emotions narrow your focus to the immediate loss, making it hard to see the bigger picture.

- **Confirmation Bias:** You start seeing only the information that supports your need to recover, ignoring red flags.

Real-Life Example

Imagine you've just taken a big loss. You feel embarrassed and angry. Instead of taking a break, you immediately place another trade—this time with twice the position size. The market moves against you again, and you lose even more. Now panic sets in. You keep trading, hoping for a miracle, but the losses keep piling up. By the end of the session, you're emotionally drained and your account is severely damaged.

This scenario is all too common—and totally preventable.

How to Overcome Revenge Trading: Practical Strategies

1. Pre-Define Loss Limits

Set a daily, weekly, or session-based loss limit. If you hit it, stop trading—no exceptions. This protects your capital and gives you time to reset emotionally.

2. Step Away After a Loss

Make it a rule: After any significant loss, step away from the screen for 10–15 minutes (or longer). Go for a walk, breathe, and clear your head before considering another trade.

3. Journal Your Emotions

Keep a trading journal and record how you feel after losses. Noticing patterns can help you catch revenge urges before they take over.

4. Focus on Process, Not Outcome

Remind yourself: Your job is to execute your plan, not to recover losses instantly. Consistency over time—not one-off wins—leads to success.

5. Have a "Loss Recovery Plan"

Instead of impulsive trading, have a plan for how you'll respond to a losing streak. This might include reviewing your trades, talking with a trading coach, or taking a full day off.

6. Practice Mindfulness & Self-Compassion

Acknowledge that losses are part of trading. Treat yourself with kindness, not criticism. Mindfulness exercises can help you observe emotions without acting on them.

7. Use Automation When Appropriate

Consider using limit orders or pre-set stops to enforce discipline, especially when emotions are running high.

8. Lean on Your Community

Share your experiences with other traders (like the SixFourTrading community). Accountability and support can make a huge difference in breaking bad cycles.

Final Thoughts

Revenge trading is one of the most destructive habits in trading—but it's also one of the most common. The key to overcoming it is self-awareness, a clear plan, and a commitment to emotional discipline. Every trader faces losses. What separates the successful from the rest is how they respond.

Remember:
You can't control the market, but you can always control your actions.
Protect your capital, protect your mindset, and give yourself permission to step back. The market will always be there tomorrow.

Revenge Trading – Cheat Sheet

Emotional Behaviors:

- Overleveraging to win it back
- Going back in immediately after stop-out

Anecdote:

"I blew 30% of my weekly gains before, because I needed to <u>feel</u> like I 'won'. That wasn't trading – it was gambling."

Solutions:

- Mandatory break after 2 red trades
- Use a Revenge Alarm (time or accountability message)
- Reframe: Losses = tuition, not betrayal

"YOU DON'T GET EVEN WITH THE MARKET. YOU GET EVEN WITH YOUR PROCESS."

CHAPTER 3

FOMO

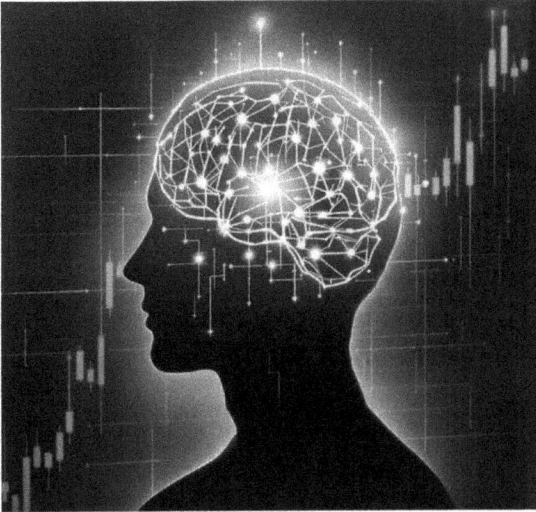

- **Chasing Trades:** Entering a trade late, after a big move, because you're afraid of missing further gains.

- **Overtrading:** Taking multiple trades in quick succession, driven by excitement or anxiety.

- **Ignoring Your Plan:** Abandoning your strategy or risk rules because "this time feels different."

- **Increasing Position Size:** Risking more than usual to "make up" for missed opportunities.

- **Reacting to Social Media:** Trading based on tips, tweets, or hype instead of your own research.

The Cost of FOMO

While FOMO might occasionally lead to a lucky win, over time, it's a recipe for inconsistency and losses. Here's why:

- **Poor Entries:** Chasing price leads to bad entry points, often right before a reversal.

- **Lack of Risk Management:** Emotional trades usually ignore stop-losses and proper position sizing.

- **Stress & Burnout:** Constantly feeling "behind" creates anxiety, which can spiral into more mistakes.

- **Erosion of Confidence:** Each FOMO-driven loss chips away at your trust in your process.

How to Overcome FOMO: Practical Strategies

Mastering FOMO is a core part of developing emotional discipline as a trader. Here's how you can tackle it head-on:

1. Have a Clear Trading Plan

Know exactly what setups you trade, your entry/exit criteria, and your risk limits. If a trade doesn't fit your plan, let it go—no matter how tempting.

2. Journal Your Emotions

Keep a trading journal and note when you feel FOMO. What triggered it? How did you react? Over time, you'll spot patterns and gain control.

3. Limit Social Media & News

Set boundaries on how often you check trading forums, Twitter, or news feeds. Curate your information sources to avoid hype and noise.

4. Practice Mindfulness

Take a few minutes before each session to center yourself. Deep breathing, meditation, or simply reviewing your plan can help you stay grounded.

5. Focus on Process, Not Outcomes

Remind yourself: Trading is about executing your strategy, not catching every move. Missing trades is part of the game—even the best traders miss out sometimes.

6. Celebrate Discipline, Not Just Profits

Acknowledge when you stick to your plan, even if it means missing a big move. Over time, this builds confidence and resilience.

7. Set Realistic Expectations

No one catches every opportunity. The market is full of endless chances—missing one is never the end.

8. Use Alerts and Automation

Set price alerts or use limit orders to help you stick to your plan, rather than reacting emotionally in the moment.

Real-Life Example

Imagine you're watching a stock that suddenly spikes after positive news. Social media is buzzing, and traders are posting huge gains. You feel the urge to jump in, even though your plan says the move is overextended. You ignore your rules, buy the top, and the stock quickly reverses—turning your excitement into regret.

Now imagine you pause, review your plan, and decide to wait for your setup. The stock pulls back as you expected. You avoided a loss and reinforced your discipline. This is the power of overcoming FOMO.

Final Thoughts

FOMO is a normal part of trading—but it doesn't have to control you. By understanding why it happens and putting practical strategies in place, you can trade with more confidence, discipline, and long-term success.

Remember: **The best opportunities come to those who wait for their edge.**

FOMO – Cheat Sheet

Emotional Behaviors:

- Jumping into trades after the move
- Following alerts blindly

Solutions:

- Use alerts, not screen-watching
- Build a 3-check confirmation: setup, structure, catalyst
- Shift identity from "hunter of moves" →"collector of edges"

CANDLE CHASING   **PATIENT SNIPER ENTRY**

DO: List 3 times FOMO cost you money + how you'd handle it now

CHAPTER 4

OVERTRADING

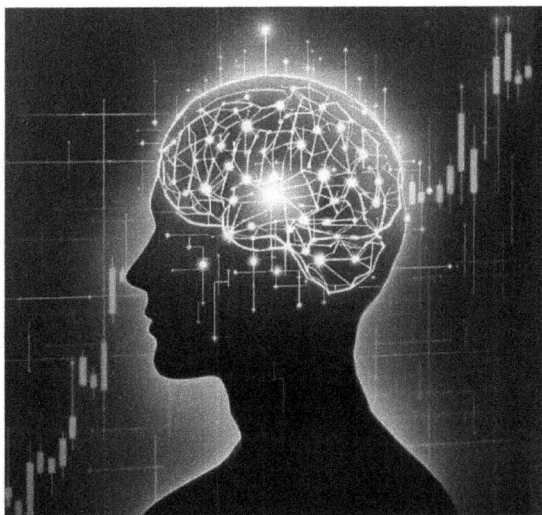

CHAPTER 4: Overtrading

What Is Overtrading?

Overtrading is the act of placing too many trades—either in frequency or size—relative to your trading plan, risk tolerance, or account size. It's a common pitfall for beginners and even experienced traders, often stemming from emotional impulses rather than sound strategy. Overtrading can take many forms: jumping into trades without clear setups, increasing position size after wins or losses, or simply trading out of boredom or the need for action.

While trading activity is essential for profit, excessive trading is usually detrimental. It leads to higher transaction costs, increased stress, inconsistent results, and, ultimately, account drawdowns or blow-ups.

Why Does Overtrading Happen?

1. Emotional Triggers

- **Boredom:** Markets can be slow, and the urge to "do something" leads to unnecessary trades.

- **Excitement:** After a win, adrenaline can push you to chase more trades.

- **Frustration:** After a loss, you might try to "make it back" quickly (often overlapping with revenge trading).

- **FOMO:** Fear of missing out can drive you to jump into every potential move, even those outside your plan.

2. Lack of a Clear Plan

Without strict rules for entries, exits, and trade frequency, it's easy to fall into the trap of overtrading. Traders without a plan often mistake activity for productivity.

3. Misunderstanding Probabilities

Some traders believe more trades equal more chances to win. In reality, more trades usually mean more exposure to risk and mistakes.

4. Desire for Quick Profits

The allure of fast money can lead traders to take every setup they see, regardless of quality or probability.

5. External Influences

Social media, chat rooms, and trading communities can create a sense of urgency and pressure to always be in the market.

How Overtrading Shows Up in Practice

- **Taking Trades Without Setups:** Entering positions that don't fit your plan or edge.

- **Increasing Trade Frequency:** Placing multiple trades in a short period, often without proper analysis.

- **Ignoring Trade Quality:** Prioritizing quantity over quality—taking any trade that "looks good" in the moment.

- **Overleveraging:** Increasing position size beyond your risk parameters to chase bigger wins.

- **Trading All Market Conditions:** Forcing trades even when the market is choppy, slow, or outside your strategy's ideal environment.

- **Chasing Losses or Wins:** Letting emotions dictate your next trade, rather than your plan.

The Cost of Overtrading

While overtrading may feel productive or exciting in the moment, it's one of the most damaging habits for traders. Here's why:

- **Increased Transaction Costs:** Every trade incurs commissions, spreads, and slippage. Over time, these eat into your profits.

- **Emotional Burnout:** Constant trading creates stress, fatigue, and decision overload, reducing your ability to make rational choices.

- **Inconsistent Results:** Overtrading leads to random results, making it hard to track your edge or improve your process.

- **Account Drawdowns:** More trades mean more opportunities for losses, especially when discipline slips.

- **Erosion of Discipline:** The more you trade outside your plan, the harder it is to stick to your rules in the future.

The Psychology Behind Overtrading

Understanding the mental drivers behind overtrading is key to overcoming it:

- **Need for Action:** Many traders equate being active with being productive. In reality, patience is often the most profitable skill.

- **Impatience:** Waiting for high-quality setups can feel uncomfortable, so traders fill the void with unnecessary trades.

- **Ego and Overconfidence:** After a string of wins, some traders feel "invincible" and start taking riskier, lower-quality trades.

- **Avoidance of Boredom or Discomfort:** Trading can become a distraction from other stresses or emotions.

Real-Life Example

Imagine you start your trading session with a clear plan: wait for a specific setup. After an hour with no trades, you get impatient. You spot a mediocre setup and take it—loss. Frustrated, you jump into another trade immediately—loss again. Now you're down for the day and desperate to recover. You keep trading, ignoring your plan, until you've taken 10 trades and blown your daily loss limit.

Had you waited for your edge, you might have taken one or two high-quality trades with a much better outcome.

How to Overcome Overtrading: Practical Strategies

1. Have a Written Trading Plan

Detail your setups, entry/exit criteria, and maximum trades per day/session. Make it clear what qualifies as a valid trade.

2. Set Trade Limits

Establish a maximum number of trades per day or week. Once you hit the limit, stop trading—even if you see another setup.

3. Use a Trading Journal

Log every trade, including the reason for entry. Over time, you'll spot patterns of overtrading and can hold yourself accountable.

4. Focus on Quality Over Quantity

Remind yourself: One high-quality trade is worth more than ten random ones. Grade your setups and only take the best.

5. Take Scheduled Breaks

Step away from the screen during slow periods. Use alarms or timers to enforce breaks and avoid trading out of boredom.

6. Review Your Performance Regularly

Analyze your trades weekly. How many were truly high-probability? What was your win rate on plan vs. off-plan trades?

7. Mindfulness and Emotional Awareness

Notice when you feel the urge to trade just to "do something." Pause, breathe, and ask if the trade truly fits your edge.

8. Lean on Community and Accountability

Share your goals and limits with other traders (like the SixFourTrading community). Accountability helps reinforce discipline.

Final Thoughts

Overtrading is a silent account killer—often fueled by emotion, impatience, and the false belief that more activity means more profit. The best traders understand that waiting for high-quality setups, sticking to a plan, and protecting their capital are what lead to long-term success.

Remember:
You don't get paid for trading more—you get paid for trading better.

Patience, discipline, and self-awareness are your most
valuable trading tools.

Overtrading – Cheat Sheet

Emotional Behaviors:

- Clicking for dopamine
- Trading every pattern, not your pattern

Anecdote:

"One week, I made 50+ trades. My account was the same, but I was mentally exhausted."

Solutions:

- Max trade rule (e.g., 3/day)
- Set a minimum R/R threshold per setup
- Use a boredom breaker checklist (gym, go for a walk, journal, work on a home project)

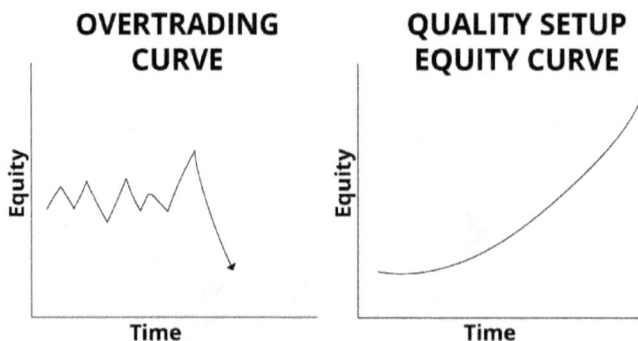

OVERTRADING CURVE — Equity vs Time

QUALITY SETUP EQUITY CURVE — Equity vs Time

CHAPTER 5

IMPATIENCE

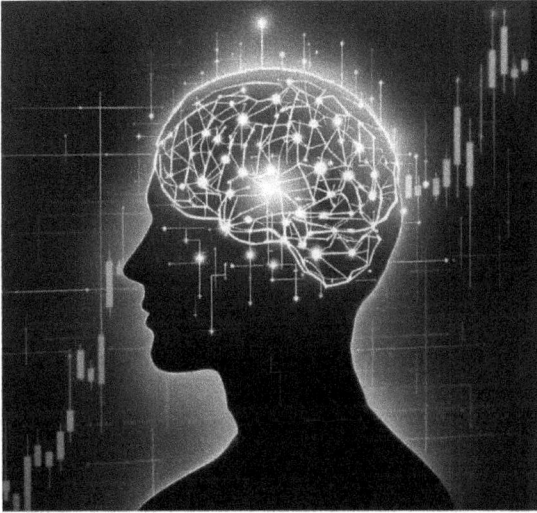

CHAPTER 5: Impatience

What Is Impatience in Trading?

Impatience is the urge to act quickly, to skip steps, or to force results before the proper conditions are met. In trading, impatience shows up as jumping into trades too early, exiting too soon, or constantly searching for action in the markets. It's the voice in your head that says, "I need to be doing something right now," even when your trading plan says otherwise.

While trading can be exciting, the reality is that high-quality setups are rare, and the best traders often spend more time waiting than acting. Impatience is a silent account killer, leading to poor decisions, unnecessary risk, and missed opportunities for growth.

Why Does Impatience Happen?

1. Desire for Instant Gratification

We live in a world of instant results—fast food, one-click shopping, real-time notifications. Trading, however, rewards those who wait for the right moment. The urge for quick wins can override the discipline needed to wait for high-probability setups.

2. Boredom and Restlessness

Markets can be slow, and waiting for your setup can feel uncomfortable. Many traders overtrade simply to fill the void, mistaking activity for productivity.

3. Fear of Missing Out (FOMO)

Impatience often pairs with FOMO—the anxiety that you'll miss a big move if you don't act now. This can cause you to chase trades or enter before your criteria are met.

4. Lack of Confidence in the Process

If you don't fully trust your trading plan or edge, you might feel compelled to take every opportunity, hoping that more trades will lead to more success.

5. Emotional Highs and Lows

Winning trades can create excitement and a sense of invincibility, while losses can trigger frustration. Both emotions can drive impatient actions, like increasing size or frequency of trades without proper analysis.

How Impatience Shows Up in Trading

- **Jumping the Gun:** Entering trades before your setup is complete or your signals align.

- **Premature Exits:** Closing trades too early out of fear or in pursuit of quick profits, missing larger moves.

- **Overtrading:** Taking too many trades in a session, often with lower-quality setups.

- **Ignoring the Plan:** Bypassing your rules because you "just want to be in the market."

- **Chasing Price:** Entering trades late, after a move has already started, because you can't wait for a pullback or confirmation.

The Cost of Impatience

Impatience may feel productive in the moment, but it's costly in the long run:

- **Lower Win Rate:** Acting before your edge is present leads to more losing trades.

- **Smaller Profits:** Exiting too early means you leave money on the table.

- **Higher Transaction Costs:** More trades mean more commissions, spreads, and slippage.

- **Increased Stress:** The constant need to act creates anxiety and mental fatigue.

- **Erosion of Discipline:** Each impatient trade
  weakens your ability to follow your plan in the
  future.

The Psychology Behind Impatience

Understanding the mental drivers of impatience is key
to changing your behavior:

- **Dopamine and Reward:** Every trade, win or lose,
  triggers a dopamine response. The brain craves
  this "hit," especially during market lulls.

- **Uncertainty Aversion:** Waiting means facing
  uncertainty. Acting, even impulsively, feels like
  regaining control.

- **Overconfidence:** After a few wins, you may
  believe you can "make it happen" whenever you
  want, skipping the patience that brought
  success in the first place.

- **Social Influence:** Watching others post wins or
  boast about "catching every move" can make
  you feel left behind, fueling impatience.

Real-Life Example

Imagine you've been watching a stock all morning, waiting for your ideal setup. The price starts to move, and you feel a surge of excitement. Instead of waiting for your confirmation signal, you jump in early—only to see the trade reverse and hit your stop. Frustrated, you enter another trade right away, hoping to make it back. By the end of the session, you've taken five trades instead of your planned two, and your results suffer.

Contrast this with patiently waiting for your setup. You take one high-quality trade, manage it according to your plan, and either win or lose with confidence—knowing you acted with discipline.

How to Overcome Impatience: Practical Strategies

1. Develop a Clear Trading Plan

Know exactly what your setup looks like and what conditions must be met before you act. Write down your rules and stick to them.

2. Journal Your Trades and Emotions

Record not just your trades, but also your feelings and impulses. Over time, you'll spot patterns and triggers for impatience.

3. Set Trade Limits

Decide in advance how many trades you'll take in a session or day. If you reach your limit, stop—even if you feel like you're "missing out."

4. Use Timers and Breaks

During quiet periods, set a timer and step away from the screen. Use this time for a walk, meditation, or reviewing your plan.

5. Celebrate Patience

Acknowledge when you wait for your setup, even if it means missing a trade. Over time, this reinforces the value of patience.

6. Focus on Process, Not Outcome

Remind yourself that your job is to execute your plan, not to catch every move. Success is measured by discipline, not by the number of trades.

7. Practice Mindfulness

Take a few deep breaths before making decisions. Mindfulness can help you recognize impulses and choose your response instead of reacting automatically.

8. Stay Busy with Productive Tasks

During slow market periods, review your journal, study charts, or work on your trading education. Productive waiting beats impulsive trading every time.

Final Thoughts

Impatience is a natural human emotion, but it's one of the greatest barriers to trading success. The best traders know that waiting for high-probability setups, sticking to their plan, and protecting their capital are what lead to long-term results.

Remember:
In trading, you're paid for your patience, not your activity.
Every time you wait for your edge, you strengthen your discipline and set yourself up for consistent, sustainable growth.

Impatience – Cheat Sheet

Emotional Behaviors:

- Entering early
- Exiting before target

Solutions:

- Use alerts instead of watching every candle
- Put a sticky note on your monitor or desk saying, "*I will follow my process.*" Repeat that to yourself out loud at least 3 times
- Take a deep breath and visualize yourself following your process

"The market pays patient traders and taxes impulsive one."

DO: Write out the full lifecycle of a perfect trade, from prep to exit

CHAPTER 6

ATTACHMENT TO TRADES

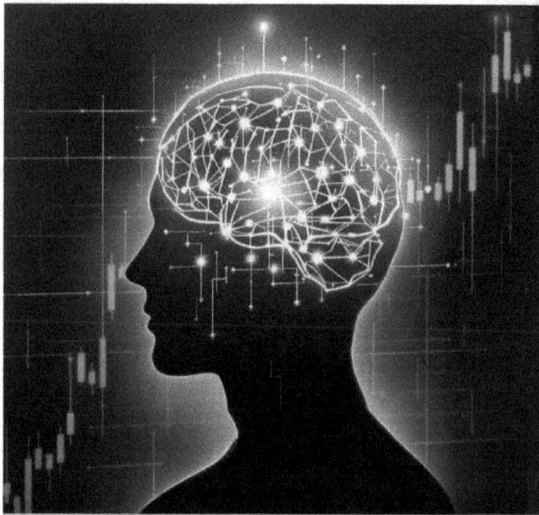

CHAPTER 6: Attachment to Trades

What Is Attachment to Trades?

Attachment to trades is the emotional investment a trader develops toward a specific position or idea in the market. Instead of treating each trade as just one of many in a long career, an attached trader becomes fixated—hoping, wishing, and sometimes even praying for a particular outcome. This attachment can manifest as an unwillingness to cut losses, holding onto winners too long, or ignoring signals that contradict your initial thesis.

Attachment is subtle but powerful. It shifts your focus from objective analysis and disciplined execution to emotional decision-making. As a result, even the best trading strategies can fail when attachment clouds your judgment.

Why Does Attachment to Trades Happen?

1. Ego and Identity

Many traders subconsciously tie their sense of self-worth or intelligence to being "right" in the market. When you become attached to a trade, it's no longer just about the money—it's about proving yourself.

2. Time and Effort Invested

The more analysis, research, or anticipation you put into a trade, the harder it is to let go. You feel like you "deserve" a positive outcome because of the effort you've invested.

3. Desire for Certainty

Markets are uncertain by nature, but attachment offers the illusion of control. Believing strongly in a trade can feel comforting—even when the market disagrees.

4. Fear of Missing Out or Regret

Letting go of a trade too soon and then watching it move in your favor can be painful. To avoid this regret, some traders cling to positions, hoping for a turnaround.

5. Recency Bias

If a particular setup worked well in the past, you may become overly confident and attached to similar trades, regardless of current market conditions.

How Attachment Shows Up in Trading

Attachment can manifest in many ways, often without you realizing it:

- **Ignoring Stop-Losses:** Refusing to exit losing trades because you "know it will come back."

- **Averaging Down:** Adding to losing positions in the hope of a reversal.

- **Overstaying Winners:** Holding onto profitable trades too long, hoping for even more, and risking a reversal.

- **Filtering Out Contradictory Information:** Only seeing data that supports your original idea, while ignoring warning signs.

- **Emotional Rollercoaster:** Experiencing intense anxiety, hope, or frustration based on a single trade's outcome.

The Cost of Attachment to Trades

Attachment is costly in both tangible and intangible ways:

- **Larger Losses:** Refusing to cut losing trades can turn small setbacks into account-damaging losses.

- **Missed Opportunities:** While fixated on one trade, you may overlook better setups elsewhere.

- **Inconsistent Results:** Emotional decisions lead to inconsistent execution, undermining your trading plan.

- **Increased Stress:** Worrying about a single trade leads to anxiety and mental fatigue.

- **Erosion of Discipline:** The more you let attachment guide your actions, the harder it becomes to follow your plan in the future.

The Psychology Behind Attachment

Understanding the psychological drivers is key to overcoming attachment:

- **Sunk Cost Fallacy:** The more you've invested (time, effort, or money), the harder it is to let go—even when it's the right decision.

- **Confirmation Bias:** You seek out information that confirms your belief in the trade and ignore conflicting data.

- **Hope and Fear:** Hope keeps you in losing trades; fear of regret keeps you from taking profits.

- **Need for Validation:** Being "right" feels good, and attachment is often about seeking validation from the market.

Real-Life Example

Imagine you've spent hours researching a stock, convinced it's about to break out. You enter the trade, but instead of rising, the price starts to fall. Rather than cutting your loss at your pre-set stop, you hold on— telling yourself the market is just "shaking out weak hands." The loss grows. You double down, convinced your research can't be wrong. By the time you finally exit, the loss is much larger than planned, and your confidence is shaken.

Contrast this with the trader who sets a stop, follows their plan, and views each trade as just one of many. They exit when the trade doesn't work and move on, emotionally detached and ready for the next opportunity.

How to Overcome Attachment: Practical Strategies

1. See Each Trade as Just One of Many

Remind yourself that no single trade determines your success. Trading is a game of probabilities, not certainties.

2. Have a Clear Trading Plan

Predefine your entry, exit, and risk management rules. Commit to following them, regardless of how you feel about a particular trade.

3. Use Hard Stops and Take-Profits

Let your plan—not your emotions—decide when to exit. Place stop-losses and take-profit orders as soon as you enter a trade.

4. Journal Your Emotions

Record your feelings before, during, and after each trade. Over time, you'll spot patterns and triggers for attachment.

5. Practice Mindfulness

Take a few deep breaths before making decisions. Notice when you feel overly invested in a trade and ask yourself why.

6. Focus on Process, Not Outcomes

Measure your success by how well you follow your plan, not by whether any single trade wins or loses.

7. Limit Position Size

Smaller positions make it easier to stay objective and less likely to become emotionally attached.

8. Debrief and Review

After each week or month, review your trades. Did attachment affect your decisions? How can you improve next time?

Final Thoughts

Attachment to trades is a silent saboteur—subtle, persistent, and deeply human. The best traders understand that success comes from disciplined execution, emotional detachment, and a focus on the long game. By recognizing attachment and putting practical strategies in place, you can trade with greater clarity, objectivity, and long-term consistency.

Remember:
The market doesn't care about your hopes or opinions. It rewards discipline, self-awareness, and the ability to move on.

Attachment to Trades – Cheat Sheet

Emotional Behaviors:

- Not cutting losers
- Talking yourself into staying

Anecdote:

"I named this well-known meme stock. I was <u>attached</u> to it. The market did not care – I lost 10%."

Solutions:

- Use trade ID's (Setup 1(S1), Setup 2(S2), etc...)
- Use automatic exits (OCO or trailing stops)
- Journal "Why I entered", "What strategy did this fit?"

TRADE IDENTITY	TRADE OBJECTIVITY
Attached	Detached
Entitled	Unbiased
Defensive	Rational
Fragile	Resilent

DO: Write down your emotional state when trading.

CHAPTER 7

CONFIDENCE ROLLERCOASTER

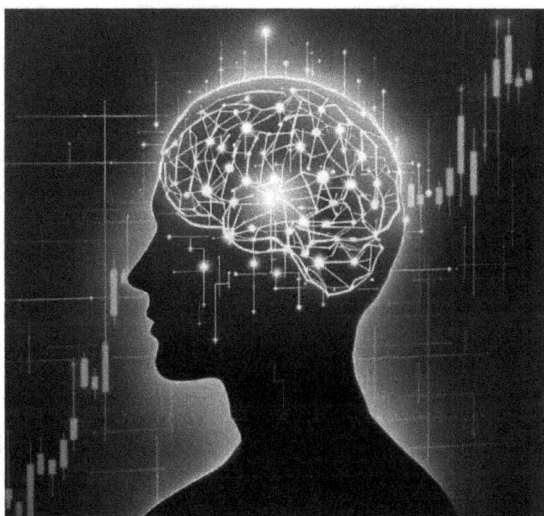

CHAPTER 7: Confidence Rollercoaster

What Is the Confidence Rollercoaster?

The "confidence rollercoaster" describes the emotional ups and downs traders experience as their confidence swings between extremes—soaring after a string of wins, plummeting after a series of losses. Instead of maintaining steady self-belief, traders on this rollercoaster find their mindset and decisions dictated by recent outcomes, leading to inconsistent performance and emotional exhaustion.

This phenomenon is incredibly common—even among experienced traders. The constant fluctuation between overconfidence and self-doubt can sabotage your trading plan, erode discipline, and make it difficult to achieve long-term success.

Why Does the Confidence Rollercoaster Happen?

1. Outcome-Dependent Self-Worth

Many traders unconsciously tie their confidence to their most recent trades. A few wins can make you feel

invincible, while a losing streak can make you question
your abilities and strategy.

2. Recency Bias

Our brains naturally give more weight to recent events. If
your last few trades were winners, you may feel on top
of the world; if they were losers, you might feel like
nothing works.

3. Lack of Process Focus

When traders focus on results instead of process, every
outcome feels like a verdict on their skill. This leads to
emotional whiplash with every win or loss.

4. Perfectionism

The unrealistic expectation of always being right in the
market creates pressure. Any loss is seen as a failure,
causing sharp drops in confidence.

5. Comparison with Others

Watching other traders' highlight reels on social media
can distort your perception, making you feel less
competent during your own drawdowns and artificially
boosting your ego during hot streaks.

How the Confidence Rollercoaster Shows Up in Trading

- **Overconfidence After Wins:**
  You increase position size, take riskier trades, or abandon your plan because you "can't lose."

- **Paralysis After Losses:**
  You hesitate to enter trades, second-guess yourself, or avoid trading altogether out of fear.

- **Chasing Losses:**
  Trying to "win back" confidence by forcing trades after a losing streak, often leading to more losses.

- **Swinging Between Extremes:**
  One week you're aggressive and bold; the next, you're cautious and withdrawn.

The Cost of the Confidence Rollercoaster

The emotional instability caused by the confidence rollercoaster can have serious consequences:

- **Inconsistent Execution:**
  Your trading decisions become driven by emotion rather than logic or a proven process.

- **Increased Risk:**
  Overconfidence can lead to oversized positions and risk exposure beyond your comfort zone.

- **Missed Opportunities:**
  Self-doubt may cause you to skip valid setups or
  exit trades too early.

- **Burnout:**
  The constant emotional swings drain your
  mental energy, making trading feel exhausting
  and unsustainable.

- **Erosion of Discipline:**
  Each emotional reaction to wins or losses chips
  away at your ability to stick to your plan.

The Psychology Behind the Rollercoaster

- **Ego and Identity:**
  Tying your identity to your trading results makes
  every win or loss feel personal.

- **Short-Term Focus:**
  Focusing on immediate outcomes rather than
  long-term performance amplifies emotional
  swings.

- **Need for Validation:**
  Seeking external proof of your skill from every
  trade outcome, instead of trusting your process.

Real-Life Example

Imagine you've just had three winning trades in a row.
You feel unstoppable, so you double your position size
on the next trade—only to take a big loss. Suddenly,
your confidence crashes. You skip the next setup, afraid
to lose again, only to watch it play out perfectly without
you. Frustrated, you chase the next trade impulsively,
leading to another loss. The cycle continues, with your
confidence rising and falling based on each individual
result.

Contrast this with a trader who measures success by
how well they follow their plan, regardless of individual
outcomes. Their confidence remains steady, and their
results become more consistent over time.

**How to Overcome the Confidence Rollercoaster:
Practical Strategies**

1. Detach Confidence from Outcomes

Remind yourself that a single trade does not define your
skill. Focus on executing your plan and managing risk—
confidence should come from discipline, not short-term
results.

2. Track Process, Not Just P&L

Keep a journal that records not just wins and losses, but how well you followed your process. Celebrate disciplined execution, even on losing trades.

3. Set Realistic Expectations

Accept that drawdowns and losing streaks are normal. No trader wins all the time. Normalize losing as part of the game.

4. Limit Position Size During Highs and Lows

Avoid increasing risk after a winning streak or cutting risk to zero after losses. Stick to your pre-defined risk parameters.

5. Review Your Trades in Batches

Analyze your performance over 20 or 50 trades, not one or two. This helps you see the bigger picture and smooth out emotional swings.

6. Practice Mindfulness

Notice when your emotions are running high or low. Take breaks, breathe, and avoid trading when you're not in a balanced state.

7. Lean on Community and Mentorship

Share your experiences with other traders. Accountability and support can help you regain perspective and avoid emotional extremes.

Final Thoughts

The confidence rollercoaster is a natural part of the trading journey, but it doesn't have to control you. By shifting your focus from outcomes to process, building self-awareness, and sticking to your plan, you can achieve the steady confidence that leads to long-term trading success.

Remember:
True confidence comes from discipline, self-awareness, and consistency—not from your last trade.

Confidence Rollercoaster – Cheat Sheet

Emotional Behaviors:

- Overconfidence →Overleverage
- Self-doubt →No Trades

Solutions:

- Track process, not profits (score checklist)
- Use a daily confidence rating (1-10)
- Stick to risk rules even after wins

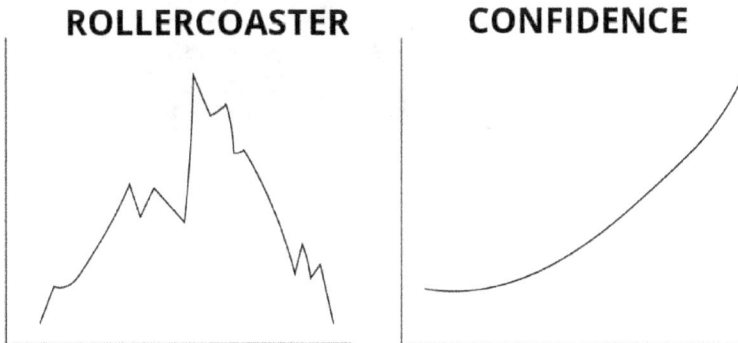

ROLLERCOASTER

CONFIDENCE

CHAPTER 8

TRADING EGO

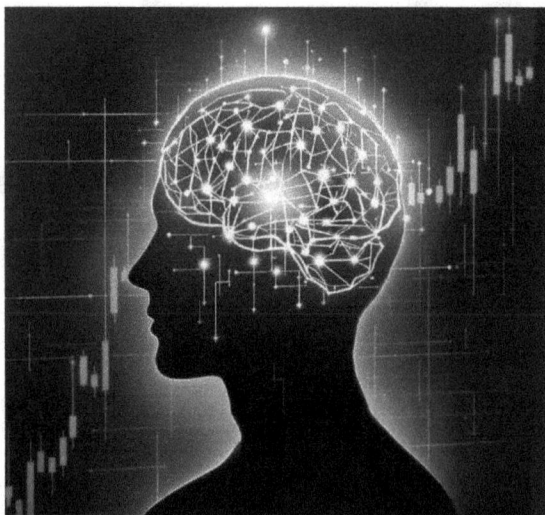

CHATPER 8: Trading Ego

What Is Trading Ego?

Trading ego is the set of beliefs, attitudes, and emotions tied to your self-image as a trader. It's the internal voice that says, "I'm right," "I can't be wrong," or "I need to prove myself." While a healthy sense of confidence is essential in trading, ego becomes a problem when it interferes with objective decision-making, risk management, and learning from mistakes.

The trading ego can be subtle or loud. Sometimes it whispers, urging you to hold onto a losing trade because "it'll turn around." Other times, it shouts, pushing you to double down after a win because "you're on fire." Left unchecked, ego can sabotage even the most well-designed trading strategies and lead to emotional rollercoasters, inconsistent results, and significant financial losses.

Why Does Trading Ego Happen?

1. Personal Identity Tied to Trading Results

Many traders, especially those with strong competitive drives, link their self-worth to their performance. A winning trade boosts their ego; a loss feels like a personal failure.

2. Desire to Be Right

Humans naturally want to be correct. In trading, this can manifest as stubbornness—refusing to admit a mistake, ignoring stop-losses, or holding onto a losing position in hopes of being "proven right."

3. Overconfidence After Success

A string of wins can inflate your sense of skill, making you believe you have the market "figured out." This can lead to reckless trades, increased risk, and ignoring your plan.

4. Fear of Looking Foolish

Some traders fear the embarrassment of being wrong, especially if they've shared their ideas publicly. Ego resists admitting mistakes, leading to denial and avoidance.

5. Attachment to Predictions

Once you've put in the work to analyze a trade, your ego wants to see that analysis validated. You become attached to your predictions and resistant to new information.

How Trading Ego Shows Up in Practice

- **Ignoring Stop-Losses:** Refusing to exit a losing trade because you "know" it will recover.

- **Averaging Down:** Adding to a losing position to "prove" your analysis was correct.

- **Overtrading After Wins:** Feeling invincible and taking unnecessary risks or oversized positions.

- **Blaming the Market:** Refusing to take responsibility for losses, blaming "manipulation" or "bad luck" instead.

- **Avoiding Review:** Skipping post-trade analysis because it's uncomfortable to confront mistakes.

- **Disregarding Feedback:** Dismissing advice from mentors or peers, convinced you know better.

The Cost of Trading Ego

Unchecked ego is one of the most destructive forces in trading. Here's how it can hurt you:

- **Compounding Losses:** Refusing to admit you're wrong leads to bigger losses.

- **Missed Learning Opportunities:** Ego resists feedback and self-reflection, slowing your growth as a trader.

- **Inconsistent Performance:** Trading decisions become emotional, not strategic.

- **Isolation:** Ego-driven traders may alienate themselves from communities or mentors who could help.

- **Emotional Burnout:** The constant battle to be "right" creates stress, frustration, and fatigue.

The Psychology Behind Trading Ego

- **Ego Defense Mechanisms:** The mind protects itself from pain by rationalizing mistakes, denying responsibility, or projecting blame.

- **Confirmation Bias:** Ego seeks out information that supports your position and ignores evidence to the contrary.

- **Loss Aversion:** The pain of being wrong is amplified by ego, making it harder to accept small losses and move on.

- **Imposter Syndrome:** Ironically, ego can mask deep-seated insecurity—overcompensating for a fear of not being "good enough."

Real-Life Example

Imagine you've spent days researching a trade. You enter with conviction, but the market moves against you. Instead of honoring your stop-loss, your ego kicks in: "This can't be happening. I'm right—everyone else is wrong." You add to your position, hoping for a turnaround. The loss grows. You feel angry, frustrated, and desperate to save face. By the time you finally exit, the damage is much worse than if you'd simply accepted the loss and moved on.

Contrast this with a trader who sets a stop, follows their plan, and treats each trade as just one of many. They accept losses with humility, learn from mistakes, and move forward without letting ego cloud their judgment.

How to Overcome Trading Ego: Practical Strategies

1. Detach Self-Worth from Results

Remind yourself that a losing trade is not a reflection of your value as a person or trader. Focus on process over outcome.

2. Develop a Written Trading Plan

Commit to following your rules, even when your ego urges you to "prove yourself." Let your plan—not your emotions—guide your decisions.

Henry "Hank" Brown

MASTERING THE MIND: EMOTIONAL DISCIPLINE IN TRADING

3. Embrace Humility

Accept that you will be wrong—often. The best traders are those who can admit mistakes quickly and adapt.

4. Use Hard Stops and Pre-Set Risk

Remove the temptation to "fight the market" by automating your exits and sticking to position sizing.

5. Regularly Review and Journal

After each session, review your trades and honestly assess where ego influenced your actions. Write down lessons learned and set goals for improvement.

6. Seek Feedback and Accountability

Share your trades and thought process with a trusted community or mentor. Outside perspectives can help you spot ego-driven decisions.

7. Practice Mindfulness

Before making decisions, pause and check in with your emotions. Are you acting from a place of logic or ego?

8. Celebrate Discipline, Not Just Wins

Reward yourself for following your plan and cutting losses—not just for profitable trades.

Final Thoughts

Trading ego is a double-edged sword. A healthy sense of confidence is vital, but unchecked ego can blind you to risk, block your growth, and wreck your account. The most successful traders are humble, self-aware, and open to learning—knowing that the market rewards discipline, not bravado.

Remember:
The market doesn't care about your ego—it only cares about your discipline and adaptability.

Trading Ego – Cheat Sheet

Emotional Behaviors:

- Needing to be right
- Ignoring invalidation signals

Anecdote:

"I held on to a trade because I knew I was right. The market didn't care, and I lost thousands."

Solutions:

- Shift from outcome-focused →process-focused
- Use humility affirmation: "I don't need to be right. I need to be consistent and stick to my process."
- Use a trading partner to sanity-check setups

"You're not fighting the market. You're fighting your ego."

DO: Write a breakup letter to your need to be right

CHAPTER 9

LACK OF CLARITY

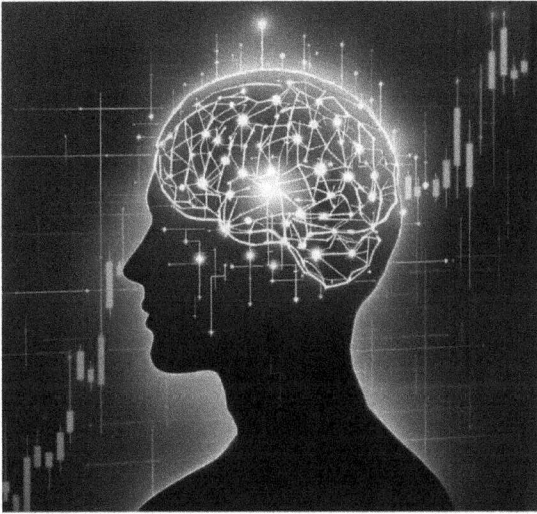

CHAPTER 9: Lack of Clarity

What Is Lack of Clarity in Trading?

Lack of clarity in trading refers to uncertainty or confusion about your trading goals, strategies, or decision-making process. It's the fog that clouds your judgment, making it difficult to act decisively or evaluate your performance. When you lack clarity, you may find yourself second-guessing trades, hesitating at crucial moments, or jumping from one strategy to another without a clear plan.

Clarity is the foundation of all successful trading. Without it, even the most talented or hardworking traders struggle to achieve consistent results. When you don't know exactly what you're aiming for or how to get there, every market move becomes stressful, and your trading journey feels chaotic rather than purposeful.

Why Does Lack of Clarity Happen?

1. Undefined Goals

If you haven't set clear, specific goals—such as your target returns, risk tolerance, or desired trading lifestyle—it's easy to drift and lose motivation. Vague aspirations like "make more money" don't provide a roadmap for daily decisions.

2. No Written Trading Plan

Trading without a documented plan is like sailing without a compass. Without clear rules for entries, exits, risk management, and position sizing, every decision is made on the fly, leading to inconsistency and confusion.

3. Information Overload

The modern trader is bombarded with news, opinions, indicators, and strategies. Trying to process everything at once can overwhelm your mind, making it hard to filter out noise and focus on what matters.

4. Strategy Hopping

Switching from one system to another after every loss or setback prevents you from mastering any approach. This constant search for a "holy grail" is a symptom of unclear objectives and a lack of trust in your process.

5. Emotional Turbulence

Strong emotions—fear, greed, frustration—cloud your judgment and make it difficult to see the market objectively. When you're emotionally reactive, your decisions become impulsive rather than clear and calculated.

6. Lack of Self-Reflection

Without regular review of your trades, strategies, and mindset, it's hard to identify what's working and what isn't. This self-awareness is essential for gaining clarity and making improvements.

How Lack of Clarity Shows Up in Trading

- **Hesitation and Indecision:** You freeze at entry or exit points, unsure if you're making the right move.

- **Inconsistent Execution:** Sometimes you follow your plan; other times you improvise, leading to unpredictable results.

- **Overtrading:** You take trades outside your strategy, hoping something will stick.

- **Second-Guessing:** You constantly doubt your analysis, often exiting trades too early or too late.

- **Strategy Switching:** You abandon your current method after a few losses, jumping to the next "hot" idea.

- **Difficulty Reviewing Performance:** Without clear benchmarks, you can't tell if you're progressing or just spinning your wheels.

The Cost of Lack of Clarity

The consequences of unclear trading are significant:

- **Missed Opportunities:** Hesitation leads to missed trades and lost profits.

- **Increased Losses:** Inconsistent execution and impulsive trades often result in bigger drawdowns.

- **Emotional Drain:** The mental fatigue of constant uncertainty can lead to stress, frustration, and burnout.

- **Stunted Growth:** Without clarity, you can't learn from your mistakes or build on your strengths.

- **Erosion of Confidence:** Each unclear decision chips away at your self-trust, making future decisions even harder.

The Psychology Behind Lack of Clarity

- **Fear of Commitment:** Committing to one strategy or goal means risking being "wrong." Some traders prefer to keep options open, but this leads to indecision.

- **Perfectionism:** Wanting everything to be "just right" before acting can prevent you from making any decision at all.

- **Need for Certainty:** The markets are inherently uncertain, but the desire for absolute clarity can lead to paralysis and over-analysis.

Real-Life Example

Imagine a trader who follows five different gurus on social media, each with conflicting advice. One says buy, another says sell, a third warns to stay out. The trader's chart is overloaded with indicators. When a setup appears, he hesitates, unsure which signal to trust. He misses the move, then jumps in late, only to get stopped out. Frustrated, he switches strategies the next day, hoping for better results—but the cycle repeats.

Contrast this with a trader who has a clear plan: one or two setups, defined rules, and a simple chart. She acts decisively, reviews her trades weekly, and knows exactly what to improve. Her results are more consistent, and her stress is lower.

How to Overcome Lack of Clarity: Practical Strategies

1. Define Your Trading Goals

Get specific. What are you trying to achieve? Monthly income, long-term growth, skill development? Write it down and revisit it often.

2. Create a Written Trading Plan

Document your entry and exit criteria, risk management rules, and daily routines. This plan is your roadmap— follow it consistently.

3. Simplify Your Strategy

Focus on mastering one or two setups. Remove unnecessary indicators and distractions from your charts.

4. Limit Information Intake

Choose a few trusted sources for news and analysis. Set boundaries on social media and avoid chasing every new idea.

5. Regularly Review Your Performance

Use a trading journal to track your trades, emotions, and decision-making. Reflect weekly on what's working and what needs adjustment.

6. Practice Mindfulness

Take a few minutes before each session to clear your mind. Deep breathing or meditation can help you focus and see the market more objectively.

7. Seek Feedback and Mentorship

Share your plan and results with a coach or community. Outside perspectives can help clarify blind spots and reinforce good habits.

Final Thoughts

Lack of clarity is an invisible barrier that holds many traders back. The path to consistent results starts with defining your goals, simplifying your approach, and committing to a process of continuous improvement. Clarity brings confidence, discipline, and the ability to act decisively—qualities that separate successful traders from the rest.

Remember:
The clearer your plan, the more confident your execution.
Every step you take toward clarity is a step toward trading mastery.

Lack of Clarity – Cheat Sheet

Emotional Behaviors:

- Hesitating
- Overanalyzing or mixing strategies

Solutions:

- Stick to 1-3 setups max
- Create a daily prep ritual (meditate, news, sentiment)
- Pre-trade checklist: conditions(catalyst), levels, bias

"THIS IS NOT A GOOD TIME TO BUY THE DIP"

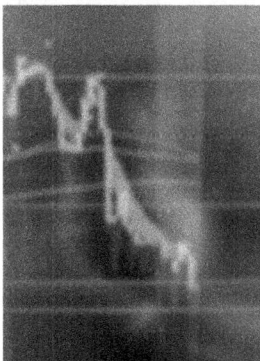

CHAPTER 10

BURNOUT & FATIGUE

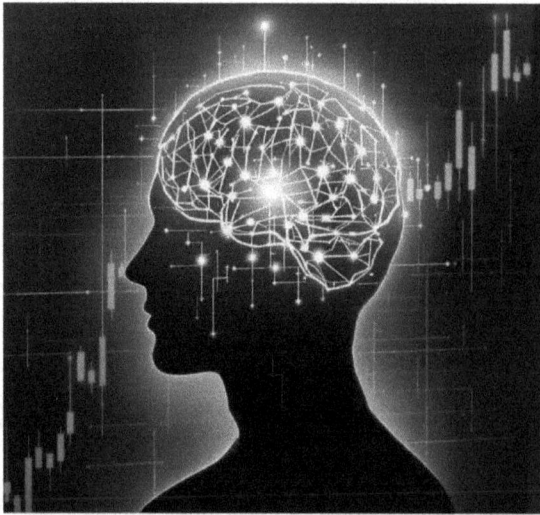

CHAPTER 10: Burnout & Fatigue

What Are Burnout & Fatigue in Trading?

Burnout is a state of emotional, physical, and mental exhaustion caused by prolonged and excessive stress. In trading, burnout often develops when you push yourself too hard, for too long, without adequate rest or balance. It's more than just feeling tired—it's a deep sense of depletion that can leave you feeling detached, unmotivated, and cynical about your trading and your goals.

Fatigue is the physical and mental tiredness that comes from overextending yourself, whether through long trading hours, constant screen time, or emotional strain. While everyone feels tired from time to time, chronic fatigue in trading can erode your focus, discipline, and decision-making ability, setting the stage for mistakes and poor performance.

Burnout and fatigue are closely related. Fatigue is often the warning sign; burnout is what happens if you ignore those signs and keep pushing.

Why Do Burnout & Fatigue Happen in Trading?

1. High-Stress Environment

Trading is inherently stressful. The pressure to perform, manage risk, and make quick decisions—often with real money on the line—creates a constant state of alertness. Over time, this can wear you down.

2. Overtrading and Long Hours

Many traders believe that more time at the screen equals more profit. In reality, excessive trading and long hours drain your mental resources, leading to diminishing returns.

3. Emotional Rollercoaster

The emotional highs of winning and the lows of losing can be exhausting. Constantly riding this wave without emotional regulation or recovery time accelerates burnout.

4. Lack of Balance

If trading consumes your life—at the expense of sleep, exercise, relationships, or hobbies—your resilience erodes. Without balance, even small setbacks can feel overwhelming.

5. Unrealistic Expectations

Chasing perfection or expecting instant success sets you up for disappointment. The constant pressure to "always win" creates chronic stress and frustration.

6. Information Overload

The relentless flow of market data, news, and opinions can overwhelm your mind, making it hard to focus and increasing mental fatigue.

How Burnout & Fatigue Show Up in Trading

- **Loss of Motivation:** You feel indifferent about trading, struggle to start your day, or question why you're doing it at all.

- **Poor Concentration:** You find it hard to focus on charts, miss signals, or make careless mistakes.

- **Emotional Numbness or Irritability:** You stop caring about wins or losses, or you become easily frustrated and impatient.

- **Inconsistent Discipline:** Rules you used to follow become optional, leading to impulsive or reckless trades.

- **Physical Symptoms:** Headaches, insomnia, muscle tension, and digestive issues can all be signs of chronic stress.

- **Withdrawal:** You distance yourself from trading communities, mentors, or even friends and family.

The Cost of Burnout & Fatigue

Burnout and fatigue don't just impact your trading—they affect your overall well-being:

- **Declining Performance:** Fatigue leads to poor decision-making, missed opportunities, and bigger losses.

- **Increased Risk of Major Mistakes:** When you're exhausted, you're more likely to ignore your plan, overtrade, or take outsized risks.

- **Loss of Passion:** Burnout can sap your enthusiasm for trading, turning what was once exciting into a chore.

- **Health Issues:** Chronic stress increases the risk of anxiety, depression, heart problems, and other health issues.

- **Damaged Relationships:** Irritability and withdrawal can strain relationships with family, friends, and fellow traders.

The Psychology Behind Burnout & Fatigue

- **Perfectionism:** The drive to "always be on" and never make mistakes creates chronic pressure.

- **Fear of Missing Out (FOMO):** The belief that you must catch every move or opportunity keeps you glued to the screen, even when you need rest.

- **Lack of Boundaries:** Difficulty setting limits—on trading hours, screen time, or risk—leads to overextension.

- **Neglecting Self-Care:** Sacrificing sleep, exercise, or social activities for trading accelerates exhaustion.

Real-Life Example

Imagine a trader who starts out energized and passionate, spending 10+ hours a day researching, trading, and monitoring the markets. At first, results are mixed, but the trader pushes harder—staying up late, skipping meals, and neglecting exercise. After a few weeks, fatigue sets in. Mistakes become more frequent, and frustration builds. The trader feels trapped in a cycle of declining performance and growing exhaustion, eventually losing motivation and questioning whether trading is worth it.

Contrast this with a trader who sets clear boundaries, takes regular breaks, maintains a healthy routine, and prioritizes balance. This trader is more focused, resilient, and able to sustain consistent results over the long term.

How to Prevent and Recover from Burnout & Fatigue: Practical Strategies

1. Set Boundaries

Define your trading hours and stick to them. Avoid the temptation to "always be on." Give yourself permission to step away from the screen.

2. Prioritize Rest and Recovery

Make sleep a non-negotiable. Schedule regular breaks throughout your trading day. Use weekends or downtime to recharge—physically and mentally.

3. Maintain Balance

Nurture relationships, hobbies, and interests outside of trading. Balance in life supports resilience in trading.

4. Practice Mindfulness and Stress Management

Incorporate meditation, deep breathing, or mindfulness exercises into your routine. These practices help manage stress and improve emotional regulation.

5. Stay Physically Active

Regular exercise boosts energy, reduces stress, and sharpens your mind. Even a daily walk can make a difference.

6. Simplify Your Trading Approach

Reduce information overload by focusing on one or two strategies. Limit your sources of news and analysis.

7. Set Realistic Expectations

Accept that losses and setbacks are part of the journey. Focus on long-term growth, not perfection or overnight success.

8. Seek Support

Connect with trading communities, mentors, or mental health professionals if you're struggling. You're not alone, and support makes a big difference.

Final Thoughts

Burnout and fatigue are silent threats that can undermine even the most skilled traders. The key to long-term success isn't working harder—it's working smarter, prioritizing balance, and taking care of your mind and body. Remember, sustainable trading is a marathon, not a sprint.

The market will always be there tomorrow. Your health and well-being are your most valuable assets.

Burnout & Fatigue – Cheat Sheet

Emotional Behaviors:

- Overtrading on low sleep
- Making emotional decisions

Anecdote:

"My worst week happened the same week I was averaging about 3 hours of sleep."

Solutions:

- Weekly rest day
- Track sleep, hydration, exercise vs. performance
- Use Trade Sprint Blocks (4 days on, 1 day off)

MIND CAPITAL
TRACKER

EMOTION	☐	☐	☐	☐	☑
SLEEP	☐	☐	☐	☐	☐
CLARITY	☐	☐	☐	☑	☐
RESULT	☐	☐	☐	☐	☑

CONCLUSION: Becoming the Trader You Envision

Mastering the mind is the true foundation of trading success. Throughout this book, you've explored the emotional challenges that every trader faces—fear of losing, overtrading, impatience, attachment to trades, the confidence rollercoaster, ego, lack of clarity, and burnout. You've also learned practical strategies to overcome each one and build the discipline, resilience, and self-awareness that separate consistently profitable traders from the rest.

Remember, trading is not just about charts, strategies, or market knowledge—it's about understanding yourself. The greatest edge you can develop isn't a secret indicator or a flawless system, but the ability to manage your emotions, stick to your plan, and grow from every experience.

Progress in trading is a journey, not a destination. There will be ups and downs, wins and losses, but each moment is an opportunity to strengthen your mindset and your process. The most successful traders are not those who never make mistakes, but those who learn, adapt, and persist with discipline.

As you move forward, revisit the lessons in this book whenever you need clarity or motivation. Keep journaling your thoughts and trades, stay connected with a supportive community, and never stop investing in your personal growth—both as a trader and as a person.

Thank you for trusting me and SixFourTrading to be part of your journey. Remember: the market will always be there, but your mindset is your most valuable asset. Trade with clarity, courage, and discipline—and success will follow.

See you in the markets!

— Hank
CEO & Senior Trading Coach, SixFourTrading

www.ingramcontent.com/pod-product-compliance
Lightning Source LLC
Chambersburg PA
CBHW061836220326
41599CB00027B/5305